A

Handbook

of

Mutual Fund Investing:

A New Perspective,

A New Paradigm

Barry G. Dolgin

The views expressed herein are the author's. Nothing discussed in this book is meant to suggest modification of your existing investments or the addition of new investments. You are advised to consult an experienced and knowledgeable investment advisor before engaging in these actions. The data indicated and referred to herein are assumed to derive from reliable sources but the author cannot guarantee their accuracy. Past performance does not guarantee future returns and the values of past statistics are not necessarily predictive of future values of those statistics.

Once again, you are advised to consult an experienced and knowledgeable financial advisor before you take any actions in response to this book.

ACKNOWLEDGMENTS

"First things first," the saying goes. Accordingly, I would like to heartily thank the following people for their contributions to this book: My brother, Steven Dolgin, skilled mathematician and artful computer programmer, for his suggestions and consummate design work; my colleague Miranda Pagan, CRPC®, Risk Officer, for her assistance in developing my model portfolios; my colleague Gladiss McClain, Sales Development Consultant, for her assistance in guiding me through the complexities of the portfolio analysis software; and my colleague Ric McGough, Senior Vice President, for his support and encouragement.

Table of Contents

Introduction

I'd like a show of hands: Who out there crosses the street with their eyes closed? Good, I thought so. Yet people invest with their eyes closed all the time. And that could be almost as dangerous.

This book will show you not only the wisdom of keeping your eyes open during the investment process, but what to look for and focus on. Things are not always as they appear in our lives, and this is especially true in the investment realm. This theme will resonate throughout our discussion. I intend to offer you a fresh perspective on investing.

The F.S.I. process employs open-end mutual funds, with which most investors are familiar. However many of the observations will be applicable to other kinds of investments.

The core of this presentation is the process known as F.S.I., which stands for "Fund Screen Investigation." It is my proprietary process for constructing mutual fund portfolios distinguished by various levels of historical risk and return. It is based, in part, on Modern Portfolio Theory principles and statistics.

The concept of risk is central to F.S.I. and central to this presentation.

I'd like another show of hands: Who out there is ready to follow this Investigation wherever it leads?

Thank you,
Barry G. Dolgin

Chapter 1
F.S.I.: "Fund Screen Investigation"

F.S.I. ("Fund Screen Investigation") is my proprietary process for constructing mutual fund portfolios characterized by varying levels of historical risk and return. It is based, in part, on Modern Portfolio Theory (MPT) principles and statistics. It is, thus, very much a quantitative approach to investing. Yet complementing this approach, and supporting it, is a set of assumptions regarding financial markets and investor psychology. This set of assumptions constitutes, in a sense, a very specific philosophy of investing. This chapter will introduce that philosophy. Subsequent chapters will describe the three steps that comprise the Investigation itself.

***

The foundational assumption of F.S.I. that underlies the entire process, quantitatively and philosophically, is that the only thing you can control as an investor is your exposure to risk. A corollary to this assumption is that no one can consistently outguess or successfully time any market, consistently choose which sectors to overweight or underweight, or consistently outperform any index or benchmark. And, by the way, you can't even control your risk exposure unless you have some idea of where the risk has, at least historically, arisen.

You may well object that you can indeed control much of the investment process: You can allocate 20% of your investment dollars to a large-company fund, 10% to a small-company fund, 25% to an international stock fund, 10% to a Treasury bond fund, 15% to an investment grade corporate bond fund, 10% to a natural resources fund and the remaining 10% to cash. But, according to F.S.I., what you are really doing is allocating dollars to the various levels of historical risk that have characterized the above categories. As such, you can increase or decrease your risk exposures by re-allocating the above dollars within the same categories.

Also, you might add, the timing of your investments is precisely under your control: "A call to my broker, and I can go 100% to cash, or 50% cash, 50% stocks, whatever." And, once again, I would reply, "What you're really doing is adjusting your risk exposures." When you begin to conceptualize the investment process as the distribution or allocation of risk exposures, then you will begin, of necessity, concentrating on the element of risk and how it can be controlled or modulated. Or, indeed, increased. This perspective, an entirely new one for many investors, is the motive force behind F.S.I.

***

Why is it impossible to predict, with any degree of consistency, the movement of markets or, e.g., individual stocks? Surely, with extensive databases going back years, computer models or algorithms could be devised that would reliably predict stock movements. Macroeconomic data, such as interest rates, levels of employment, inflation, GDP, etc., are readily available. Company specific data, such as revenue, debt levels, cash flow, net income, etc. can be readily accessed via computerized databases. There is no lack of meaningful data. Yet the nature of the marketplace in which stocks are traded, the huge number of variables that can enter into valuation and trading decisions, and the ever-changing nature of their interaction, simply cannot be incorporated into a reliably predictable computer model, no matter how complex or responsive to ongoing, time-sensitive inputs. Some outcomes here on planet Earth simply cannot be predicted. The weather is another example. Intricate computer programs are used to model climate and weather predictions. Raise your hand if you'd like to buy 1000 shares of "Sunny and mild on Friday, winds out of the northwest at 5-10 miles per hour, high temperature 75 degrees"? I thought so.

And don't forget the human element (this being planet Earth). An increasing amount of research is being conducted on investor psychology. Fear and Greed are not easily quantifiable or predictable (though I wouldn't be surprised if someone, somewhere, isn't trying). But the human element can also be rational and deliberate. Professional money managers, sophisticated institutional investors and calculating hedge funds all have their logical analyses of markets and investment returns. Needless to say, these analyses and conclusions may be at significant odds with each other.

We are not dealing with a closed system of choices or possibilities: A deck of cards is a suitable analogy. Let's assume I'm dealing from this deck, which has been thoroughly shuffled so that the cards are randomly distributed. You and two others are receiving the cards, dealt face up. As the first recipient, we can know precisely the probability of your receiving any particular card. As additional cards are dealt, subsequent probabilities can be more finely tuned because we know precisely which cards remain undealt and remain in the deck, in a successively smaller "population." And it matters not who is dealing and who is receiving. And the sequence of the cards that have been dealt has no effect whatsoever on the sequence of the cards that remain undealt.

***

The stock market (as just one example of a securities market), is completely different in all respects. While there may be a finite number of listed stocks at any point in time, the forces acting on the disposition of these shares are infinitely more complex. The system (actually calling it a "system" implies more organization than is likely in evidence) is wide open. Inputs of all kinds are constantly intruding. These may be variables or data that affect stocks in general, or are relevant to specific industries, or just individual companies. Actually, some data may be dually (or triply) characterized: A computer company announces revenue and earnings for the last quarter well below the Street's expectations. The company's stock is duly hammered, but so are the stocks of competing companies in the same sector. The inference is that the variables that affected the former are relevant to the latter. And there are data that are clearly limited to a specific company: The company's outside auditor resigns (ohhh, the implications!), a major product is recalled for whatever reason(s), the company announces an acquisition of a competitor at a presumed exorbitant price, the company's market share has slid, etc.

By the way, company specific inputs can be positive: The company announces a share buy-back, increased market share, a dividend increase, or a revolutionary new product introduction, etc. And (who would've guessed?) some data can be variously interpreted: The company's dividend increase is bad news because it has nothing better to do with the cash, the increased market share was generated by cutting prices, and the share buy-back is being funded by an increase in debt. And don't forget the classic conundrum: The company is sitting on a generous pile of cash (good news), but this fact itself suggests that the company has the ability to use this cash for something egregiously moronic, like overpaying for a competitor (bad news).

***

The above examples are a minute sample of the (expanding?) universe of possible data points that can affect the valuation of stocks. Pick up any day's copy of the Wall Street Journal and you'll get the idea. And huge numbers of these data points seemingly arise from "left field," taking investors completely by surprise. The increasing globalization of markets, investment, and capital only increases the proliferation of potentially relevant data points. Of course, what's relevant and what's not is subject to interpretation and conjecture. The Efficient Market Hypothesis states that all available information relating to the evaluation of stocks is widely disseminated and reflected in current prices. The "Market" has decided what's relevant and what's not, and how to weight existing data. The resultant price reflects all that is presently known regarding a given stock and renders reliable and predictable above-market gains unlikely. At this point, The Random Walk Theory assumes that new data will be incorporated as they arrive, and a stock's price adjusted accordingly. But because these new data insist on occurring in a venue known as the future, they are unknowable and sometimes seemingly random, and cannot be rationally incorporated into a stock's current price. In other words, reliable, systematic outperformance of the market is really very difficult.

Let's take a look at a well-known (on Wall Street) cautionary statement, attributed to the well-known British economist John Maynard Keynes: "The market can stay irrational longer than you can stay solvent." Presumably this means that in spite of the professional investment community's intricate algorithms and complex mathematical computer models that can suggest rational valuations (prices) of securities and how these valuations (prices) may be predicted to change, unfortunately said predictions may remain subject to the whims of an irrational market. Had enough randomness and irrationality? But let's stop and think about what it means for a market to be irrational.

In order to identify an irrational market, we need, *ipso facto*, to be able to identify a rational one. But this is easier said than done. Let's ask around for some opinions: An investment bank's trading desk? The manager of a U.S. large-cap mutual fund? A hedge fund specializing in merger arbitrage? A commercial bank's trust department? A professor at a leading university economics department? It's not inconceivable that we would receive five different definitions. The ultimate irony, I would suggest, is that a rational market is undefinable, and, therefore, so is an irrational one. Is this due to the nature of securities markets and the participants therein, the perspective of the defining agent, the ever-changing macroeconomic context of an increasingly international, interconnected and interdependent marketplace, the phase of the moon, or all of the above? It's time to move on.

***

You've just been confronted with some really unpleasant news regarding Homo sapiens' ability to make reliable predictions relating to securities markets. It appears that virtually everything relating to the investment process is outside our control, limiting our ability to generate predictable outcomes. F.S.I. believes how an investor handles this news affects his/her likelihood of achieving desirable long-term investment results. It is quite difficult psychologically for many of us to adapt to, or accept, a world without enduring patterns and some semblance of predictability. Emotionally, this realization might even transcend Fear and Greed (is that possible?)! The question then becomes: "In an investment world which seems largely devoid of predictability, and in which, as investors, the only variable we can control is the extent of our risk exposure, how do we proceed?"

ANSWER: Finish the book! Because this is what F.S.I. is all about.

***

In the practice of medicine, the prime directive is "First, do no harm." In investing, as far as I'm concerned, it's "First, limit your losses." Not particularly inspirational, is it? But, nevertheless, the starting point for improving your probability of a successful long-term investment experience. It's actually all about the number system we've employed for quite a few years. If your portfolio loses 20% one year, to get back to even, it needs to rebound by 25%. No big deal? If your portfolio declines by 30%, getting back to even requires a gain of over 42%. Lose 37%, by which the S&P 500 did indeed tumble in 2008, and you must gain over 58% to get back to New Year's Eve, 2007.

Being aware of the historical risk a specific portfolio of actively managed mutual funds has generated, is the first step in attempting to limit future losses, if not prevent them. We can increase the probability of higher future losses by constructing a portfolio that has experienced higher historical risk. We can decrease the probability of higher future losses by constructing an actively managed mutual fund portfolio that has experienced lower historical risk. Notice the word "probability." We simply cannot be sure a portfolio which has avoided higher risk in the past will continue to do so. All we can do is be aware of the historical levels of risk associated with a given portfolio and assume that the judgment and expertise practiced historically will be operative to some extent in the future. There are no guarantees. If you compare two portfolios in terms of historical risk over the last three years, and portfolio A has experienced twice the risk of portfolio B over that time period, and this fact is all you know about these two portfolios, which would you choose if you wanted lower risk over the next year? I'd choose B.

You've heard the disclaimer: "Past performance is no guarantee of future returns" (or some similar variant). It has always been and will forever be thus. F.S.I. considers a constellation of variables at the levels of the individual mutual fund and the portfolio, in addition to performance.

As we shall see, risk is chief among them. Again, any conclusions we draw are subject to the analogous disclaimer: "Any conclusions drawn from past data do not guarantee the future validity of said conclusions or predictions derived from them." But that doesn't mean we should ignore the huge quantities of historical data readily available to us through readily accessible computerized databases and mutual fund web sites. That might engender yet another disclaimer: "Ignore the plethora of available data at your own peril." (I substituted "peril" for "risk" since we will be using "risk" in a very specific way as our Investigation progresses.) The real question becomes "What is the most productive way of evaluating the huge store of available historical data to assist us in selecting individual mutual funds and constructing risk-managed portfolios therefrom?" No matter how cleverly we choose mutual funds and construct portfolios comprised of them, based on historical data, we cannot assume these funds and portfolios will perform as they have historically. Yes, the preceding was another disclaimer.

Our Investigation continues with additional build-out of the philosophical platform that supports F.S.I. Any investor having but minimal experience with mutual funds is aware of the extensive array of categories available. Most often, the category is stated within the name of the fund: The ABC Large Company Growth Fund, the ABC Small Company Value Fund, the ABC Equity Income Fund, the ABC Emerging Markets Stock Fund, the ABC Balanced Fund, the ABC Asset Allocation Fund, the ABC Intermediate Bond Fund, the ABC Ultra-Short Bond Fund, the ABC Convertible Bond Fund, the ABC Multi-Cap Stock Fund, the ABC Large Company Blend Fund, the ABC Global Stock Fund, and so on. (I assume you've got the point by now.) Sometimes a given fund will stray from its titled mandate, which may be allowed, to some extent, by prospectus. Sometimes a fund strays a bit too far from its stated mandate or objective, a situation known as style drift. If you placed X dollars in a large company growth fund to have Y% exposure to that category based on a predetermined asset allocation program (generated by yourself or your advisor) you may not be achieving the planned exposure due to style drift. To the extent your other fund selections indulge in style drift, so deviates your allocation from its planned exposures.

Why might a fund drift from its stated category or objective? A glaringly obvious reason is that said category or objective is under significant pressure in the current markets, which is to say that the constituent securities are being unceremoniously sold, and the fund manager has few attractive places to hide. So he or she ventures into a related investment category which is currently experiencing more humane or positive market treatment. And who could blame him or her? If the mutual fund managers we hire to build our portfolios could drift in a timely way, and "drift back" again when the time is right, let them drift away. F.S.I. firmly believes this is impossible to do consistently. By the way, style drift is essentially eliminated in an index fund because it is not actively managed, thereby providing no opportunity for drift.

Our discussion of style drift is relevant to the extent that we propose a specific asset allocation model, with so much allocated to this category, so much to that category, and so on. Here now is the point (you've undoubtedly been waiting for one) to this discussion of mutual fund categories and asset allocation models: F.S.I. does not believe in generating specific, percentage-based asset allocation models in order to construct a portfolio. And it doesn't matter who does the generating, whether the investor or his/her financial advisor. By not adhering to a specific model generated at a specific point in time, even though it may be assumed to reflect the risk tolerances, return expectations, and time horizons of a specific investor, F.S.I. is emphasizing an investment framework that stresses flexibility.

What does all this mean in terms of mutual fund selection and portfolio construction? Because the model portfolios

F.S.I. has created are comprised of individual, pre-selected funds, let's simplify the question and concentrate on the implications for our selection of individual funds. In Chapter 3 we shall discuss the screening process relating to individual fund selection in detail. You will see that the process begins with the identification of an investment category. The choice of these categories obviously influences the selection of individual funds and, of course, the character of the ultimate portfolio. By selecting funds from categories that are intrinsically broader, such as asset allocation funds that themselves consist of various kinds of stocks and bonds, as well as cash, and multi-cap funds that can invest in companies of all sizes, as but two examples, we can achieve a degree of flexibility embedded at the level of the individual fund (by the way, the fixed-income version of the multi-cap global stock fund is the multi-sector bond fund). Also, this may enhance the potential diversification of the portfolio itself, by initiating the process at the fund level in addition to the diversification realized by choosing funds that themselves have not been highly correlated. (We will discuss diversification and correlation in more detail in Chapter 4.) Understand too, that when F.S.I. has certain specific goals in mind, more tightly focused funds are indeed appropriate. This is particularly the case when a specific fund focused on a historically low-risk category is added to a portfolio to reduce risk, or conversely, when a specific fund focused on a historically higher-risk category is used to increase risk and thereby increase the potential of higher return. Philosophically, the F.S.I. process is predisposed toward flexibility in the individual funds it employs.

The portfolio is what F.S.I. is ultimately about. Individual funds are carefully selected through a disciplined screening process, but they represent the building blocks that create the final unit of analysis: the portfolio. There are two broad kinds of portfolios, distinguished by objective: growth and income. As of this writing F.S.I. has constructed three growth portfolios and two income portfolios. These can be weighted in multiple ways based on risk tolerance and return expectations, resulting in innumerable combinations. But the primary consideration remains historical level of risk. This follows, of course, from the foundational assumption referred to previously, that the only factor we can control as investors is our exposure to risk. A quick lesson in the astronomy of risk should clarify the matter: In our solar system, as currently constituted, the planets revolve around the star known as the Sun, each planet maintaining its customary orbit. In the system conceptualized by F.S.I., my portfolios revolve around the star known as Risk, each maintaining its own historically characteristic distance. The mission of the F.S.I. process is to provide investors with risk-based and risk-managed vehicles designed to enable them to navigate their journey of wealth accumulation on their own individualized course, never forgetting that the star known as Risk exerts a powerful gravitational attraction.

Chapters 3, 4, and 5 will present the three steps of the F.S.I. process. But first, in Chapter 2, we must explore the nature of Risk in some detail. Raise your hand if you're ready.

Chapter 2
Measuring Risk

Because Risk plays so central a role in the F.S.I. process, it seems prudent to devote an entire chapter to examining what we mean by Risk, and how we measure it. (By the way, from now on Risk will be referred to with a capital "R," as befits its role. I reserve the right to resort to all caps, should the context so demand.) You may have your own definition of Risk, even perhaps a very personal one. It might interest you to see how closely yours resembles that of F.S.I. In any case, F.S.I. uses the term as it is generally employed by investment analysts and the Street. And this leads us to the statistic that measures Risk and, by so doing, defines it: Standard Deviation (SD). This is a statistic much referred to in Modern Portfolio Theory.

You may be in for a bit of a surprise. SD actually measures variation, or dispersion, of a group of numbers from the mean or average of those same numbers. These numbers may be expressed in virtually any unit, but do not include so-called ordinal numbers, that is, numbers that are used to establish rank, such as first, second, and third. Obviously, for our purpose, the unit is percent. As in the 3-year return of fund ABC was 7.5% annualized, and the 3-year return of portfolio XYZ was 5% annualized. The SD will be expressed in the same units as the numbers used as inputs for calculation, in this case, percent. But we may also calculate a SD for the heights of men in the age group 15-30, represented by a randomly chosen sample. These numbers can be expressed in inches, and the SD will also be expressed in inches. We could compare this SD with one derived from a measurement of the heights of a randomly chosen sample of women ages 15-30, and see which sample has more variation in height. We could compare the home run production of the New York Yankees from 1990 through 2000, on an annual basis, with that of the New York Mets from the same years, to see which team had more annual variation in production. The inputs would be number of home runs, and the SD would be expressed in home run units. And so on. The higher the SD, the more variation in the group of numbers from its mean.

The glaringly unavoidable question for us now is "How does a statistic that measures degree of variation serve also as a measure of Risk?" The answer follows:

Let's consider two hypothetical mutual funds: A and B. We'll be looking in particular at the previous 5 years' quarterly returns, for a total of 20 data points. Let's assume the distribution of fund A's returns around its average is much broader than fund B's around its average. In other words, there is quite a lot more variation in A's returns than B's, at least for the 5 years being considered. The actual numbers are not important for our purpose. But assuming you knew them, could you guess the return for the next quarter, which starts today (whenever that is), for each of the funds? Of course not! No matter how much data we may have access to, we still cannot predict future performance. So, for our purpose, the real question becomes: "For which fund, A or B, would you have a higher *probability* of being closer to the actual return, if you guessed the respective average (using this number would seem to be a reasonable approach) of the previous 20 quarters as the return for the next quarter for each fund?" Think about it. Remember, we're dealing with relative probabilities, not certainties. By the way, the larger variation of fund A's returns indicates a higher SD.

The answer is B. The narrower range of returns over the last 5 years would suggest (not guarantee), everything else being equal, that the next quarter's return would more likely fall in a narrower range than fund A's next quarterly return, therefore closer to the average of the previous 20 quarters. Therefore, we have somewhat more predictability with fund B than with fund A, in terms of approximating future quarterly returns. To the extent that we have more predictability with fund B than fund A, we are, in a sense, taking less Risk with fund B than fund A. The narrower the historical range of values (returns, heights, number of home runs, etc.) in a sample or population of values, the more confidence we can have in estimating future values, everything else being equal. The more confidence we have in an estimate of a future value, the fewer surprises we should encounter when that value becomes known. Fewer surprises means more predictability and less Risk.

So we have the following progressions: Higher historical variation (higher SD) = less predictability = more Risk, and lower historical variation (lower SD) = more predictability = less Risk.

And there you have it. This is how a statistic which directly measures variation can be considered to be a measure of Risk as we use the term in analyzing investments.

A handy feature of SD as a measure of Risk is that values are directly comparable. That is, a mutual fund with a 3-year annualized SD of 15% has been twice as risky as a fund with a 3-year annualized SD of 7.5%. This comparability obtains even when SD's of funds from different investment categories are the subject. We can directly compare the SD of a given stock fund with a given bond fund in a meaningful way.

The specificity and comparability provided by the use of this statistic is extremely valuable. By the way, as we shall see, it also applies to Risk valuations at the portfolio level. We can directly compare portfolios with each other by historical Risk and also compare portfolios with various indexes in terms of historical Risk. Also, you may have heard of another so-called Modern Portfolio Theory statistic called beta, also regarded as a measure of Risk. Beta measures volatility of a mutual fund (or stock) relative to an appropriate index, that is, an index which is assumed to represent the category in which the mutual fund specializes. Beta indicates whether the fund itself has been historically more or less volatile than the underlying index. Assume you're screening for the most attractive fund(s) in a given category, and beta is a variable you deem relevant. You proceed to identify a fund that has outperformed its underlying index over the last year, with a lower beta. Good news! But let's further assume that the category you've chosen is small-company growth stocks, an intrinsically risky category. By finding a fund with a lower beta, you may still be exposing yourself to significant Risk, simply because being less risky than a high-Risk category doesn't mean that you're courting low Risk, just *lower* Risk.

F.S.I. much prefers SD as a measure of Risk because it is an absolute measure, not a relative one. It is this characteristic that enables us to make meaningful comparisons between and among funds that specialize in vastly different investment categories, as mentioned earlier. Excuse this digression, but when it comes to understanding Risk, we must follow our Investigation wherever it leads.

Chapter 3
F.S.I.: Initial Screening

Our Investigation continues with an examination of the first step of the F.S.I. process: the initial screening. The purpose here is to select the most attractive fund(s) within a given investment category. As this chapter progresses, it will become obvious what I mean by "attractive." This step actually consists of two phases. The first phase employs mutual fund screening software that accesses a database consisting of thousands of individual funds (associated share classes are treated as separate entities) and offers dozens of variables to screen against. The second phase involves a visit to the respective web sites of the funds that survive phase one. Here we seek additional evidence that will allow us to finish the first step with one or two final choices. (Our inspection of these web sites does not require a search warrant.) This first step, repeated over any number of investment categories, provides the individual funds that comprise my portfolios.

We begin with an example of a phase one screen. The software updates its database monthly. The data used here are as of 9.30.2010. I have chosen the investment category of "large-cap growth." Funds in this category are assumed to focus mainly on U.S. companies. The database indicates that 1467 funds met this initial criterion. Remember that this number counts multiple share classes of the same fund as separate entities.

Now comes the fun part. We invest to make money, so it seems only fitting to begin the screening process with total return at NAV, or net asset value. This statistic is expressed as a percent and includes reinvestment of dividends and capital gains, if any, over the period chosen. The use of NAV excludes sales charges from consideration, so all funds begin on a level playing field, so to speak. This database includes so-called no-load funds. The F.S.I. process normally covers a 3-year period for all variables used in phase one. This timeframe provides some historical perspective as well as more recent exposures. Because of the dismal showing in 2008 (S&P 500 down 37% on a total return basis), I begin with a rather conservative choice for our first return hurdle: greater than or equal to (≥) 0% annualized for the last 3 years as of 9.30.2010. We find 22 funds met this criterion. Wanting a larger base to consider, I lowered the hurdle to ≥ -5%, and 464 funds cleared it. That's too many, so I raised the hurdle to ≥ -2.5% and we are left with 128 funds. Remember, these numbers may include multiple share classes of the same fund, and cover the trailing 3 year period. We now introduce a second variable, or statistic.

It is the introduction of a specific Risk variable that, while I suspect not entirely unique to F.S.I., nevertheless distinguishes it. Obviously, the variable is standard deviation (SD). We begin with a higher level and work toward lower levels (the opposite of our series of performance or return hurdles). In this particular case, I began with an SD of less than or equal to (≤) 25%. Of the 128 funds remaining, 61 cleared this hurdle. We raise the hurdle by lowering our SD requirement to ≤ 22.5% and 39 funds fall by the wayside, leaving us with 22. Let's add another hurdle.

It's manager tenure. After all, it's the manager who is ultimately responsible for making the buy and sell decisions regarding the securities in the fund. When you choose a mutual fund, you are really choosing a manager. I want him or her to have been around for a comparable period to that used for the other variables. Needless to say, I screen for a tenure of equal to or greater than 3 years. We lose 8 funds. When we eliminate additional share classes of the same fund, we are left with 9 different funds. You'll remember we started with 1467. I like to enter phase two with no more than 4 or 5 funds. By re-examining the stats of the remaining 9, we can eliminate additional funds, i.e. we can eliminate some of the riskiest remaining funds, and/or those lagging in performance. This is a matter of personal preference.

Indeed, the original levels we set for return and Risk are also matters of personal preference and judgment. We may want to restrict our Risk level to something under the 3 year SD of an index, say the S&P 500. We may be satisfied with performance somewhat less than that of the same index. This is where the experience, expectations, and judgment of the investor and/or the financial advisor enter the picture. It is sorely tempting to say phase one is completely objective, strictly by the numbers. But where to begin setting the heights of the respective hurdles does allow a degree of subjectivity to emerge. This is not necessarily a bad thing.

By the way, if things are still too close to call with our remaining 9 funds, we can add an additional variable. R-squared is one I find relevant. It is another Modern Portfolio Theory statistic (you can have this variable printout in your results by simply asking your database to display all funds with an R-squared ≥ to 0). It measures to what degree the returns of a given fund are related to the returns of an appropriate comparison index. Its value ranges between 0 and 1. The higher the number, the more highly related the fund's returns are to the index (this aspect of relativity to an underlying index recalls our discussion of beta in chapter 2). In other words, the higher the R-squared, the more the movement of the index will account for the movement of the fund, for the time period in question. Why R-squared? As a fund's R-squared approaches 1, more and more of the variation of its returns can be accounted for by the returns of the underlying index. If this relationship obtains for an extended period, we may be looking at the proverbial "closet index fund." However, an actively managed fund has a higher management fee than an index fund, and particularly an ETF. If you want to track an index, buy an index fund or ETF. The F.S.I. process prefers some creative thinking from its managers (as long as the Risk is not unduly inflated) and is prepared to pay for it. Again, let me emphasize that even though phase one relies on a series of values of particular statistics, there is still an element of subjectivity. Again, let me emphasize that this is not necessarily a bad thing. On to phase two!

***

In phase two we visit the respective web sites of the survivors of phase one and drill down to the specific fund. You will notice that the various share classes of each fund are available on the web site. Generally, it should not make much difference which one you investigate. When it comes to the actual buying decision, share class does make a difference (you and/or your financial advisor should research the various options to choose one appropriate for your own situation). Our Investigation here is in search of a number of clues to assist us in our final decision. The following discussion does not presume to include all the clues that may be relevant from time to time, depending on the particular screen. Much of the data we will examine are updated quarterly or monthly, depending on the fund family. Also, the following discussion will not deal specifically with the actual funds that survived phase one. It is my intention to provide a more generalized discussion of phase two, to emphasize the fact that each screen is different, with its own unique characteristics.

One of the first bits of data I look at is the relative weighting of the top 10 individual positions. In the case of stock funds, this is usually a list of stocks with percentage weighting as a function of total assets. Cash and/or other non-stock securities may appear here. I want to know what percentage of the entire portfolio is included in the top 10 positions. Is the portfolio heavily weighted in these positions? Does any given position command a relatively large share of the assets? How many total positions are included in the portfolio? Some funds may have a total of only 25 or so individual positions and I want to know this. A fund with 25 positions may be riskier than one with 50 or 75. This fact itself however would not necessarily result in the exclusion of the former. Don't forget, it would have survived phase one in which we specifically screened for Risk. But we want to take note of the degree of concentration in any case. This applies as well to our next clue.

It is sector concentration: the percentage of assets in the top 10 sectors of the fund. For example, is 25% of the fund in technology stocks and another 25% in financial stocks? We cannot know if these weightings will be advantageous, even though we may have our own ideas of which sectors should be overweight at this time. But, presumably, placing 50% of the assets in just 2 sectors could only increase Risk, rather than modulate it. Make a note.

Another variable accessible on a fund's web site, and worth knowing, is the size of the fund in dollars. Here we must be careful to include all share classes to arrive at an accurate number. Why does size matter? A larger fund has less flexibility with regard to investing future cash flows into the fund. In order for additional purchases of securities to move the needle, so to speak, increasingly large positions must be accumulated either in existing holdings or new ones. The latter may not be so easy to find, if the manager's best ideas have already been funded. Furthermore, if the fund specializes in securities, such as many small company stocks, that may be thinly traded, deploying large amounts of new cash may progressively push up a new purchase's price on the buy side, and progressively depress the price on the sell side if the manager decides to exit the stock. In fact, it is not uncommon to see small company stock funds that have attracted significant inflows because of superior performance, close to new investors (generally existing holders can make additional purchases). F.S.I. has a preference for smaller funds, all else being equal (or close to equal).

One additional note regarding size. It is conceivable that for whatever reason, the fund may be so small that in order to cover costs, the expense ratio may be unusually high as a percentage of assets. This is definitely worth noting. High expense ratios, though they may trend lower as a percentage as the fund gains additional assets, are generally best avoided, all else being equal (or close to equal).

By the way, it should be added here that if, in phase one, we were able to reduce the survivors sufficiently without resorting to R-squared, then here in phase two it may make sense to revisit this statistic.

I debated with myself whether to include the paragraph you are now reading. It directs your Investigation toward discovering the process by which the manager of the fund chooses securities to buy and to sell. What factors are important in this determination? How does he/she evaluate the securities under consideration? Do not expect to observe the following (or some variant thereof): "We screen our extensive database to uncover the most over-valued stocks we can find." In other words, expect to discover that the manager employs a rational, systematic, and objective process. That's a shocker! Clearly, whatever process is employed has landed the fund in the list of finalists. Nevertheless, I still like to take a look. Just curious, I suppose.

***

Before we continue, a caveat. Phase one of the initial screening process began with a specific investment category. Whatever database you use for this phase should limit consideration to funds which it has so labeled. But any given fund that we further investigate in phase two, on the fund company's web site, may label itself differently. In our screen, for example, we chose large-company growth funds. But it would not be inconceivable if the web site of one of the survivors labeled it as a large-company blend fund, meaning that it could include both growth and value stocks. You may also find, as you extend your Investigation, that the fund can hold mid-size and small company stocks, as well as large. Try and get a feel for the various categories of investments that the fund can hold, and indeed, what categories it does hold as of the latest update. If you find differing classifications from your original selection, my preference is to go with the one you find on the web site. In other words, you may want to remove the fund from consideration as a member of the existing screen category, and/or re-screen using a more appropriate category.

***

There are any number of ways for a manager to modulate Risk in a fund, be it stock, bond, or balanced. Rather than creating a detailed list, which would in any case almost certainly not be exhaustive, I would refer you to the paragraphs above that discuss position and sector weightings. If the investment category is international stocks, I would also examine the country weightings. If the category is multi-sector bonds, I would check to determine to what extent the portfolio includes different kinds of bonds. We could broaden this discussion to include numerous other categories of funds, but the point is this: Diversification lessens Risk. There are other techniques beyond diversification. As you gain experience in finding managers who have a decent track record in the Risk management realm, you'll discover them. By the way, I'm inclined to avoid a manager who feels he/she must outperform his/her peer group at any cost, and is prepared to assume additional Risk to do so. I've devoted a separate paragraph to the Real Story, the Real Bottom Line. It follows immediately.

If the manager of the fund is not specifically concerned with managing Risk, chances are it may not happen. I want to see a manager who is sensitive to the myriad ways Risk can creep into a portfolio, and who is constantly sensitive to its presence. Talking about modulating Risk and actually taking specific steps to accomplish it are two entirely different matters. But we don't have to guess at a manager's sincerity or his/her ability in this regard. Remember standard deviation (you needn't raise your hand)?

***

In the next chapter, our Investigation focuses on correlation and the correlation matrix. This is ultimately about diversification. Which is to say, we give it the attention it deserves.

Chapter 4
F.S.I.: The Correlation Matrix

In the context of F.S.I., correlation is to diversification as standard deviation is to Risk. That is, correlation allows us to quantify the extent of diversification just as standard deviation allows us to quantify Risk.

The correlation coefficient, represented by the letter "r" (you guessed it, R-squared derives therefrom), can range in value from -1 to +1. It measures the extent to which two variables or values track each other. The more closely the two variables move together, in the same direction, the more closely r approaches +1. The more closely the two variables move together, but in opposite directions, the more closely r approaches -1. A correlation of zero means that the two variables are entirely unrelated, like successive flips of a coin. Each flip says absolutely nothing about the next one (or the one before).

F.S.I. uses r to express the correlation between the returns of two mutual funds for a given time period. When dealing with a set of funds for which we want to examine the correlations between all possible fund pairings, a so-called matrix is a common format. Figures 1 and 2 illustrate sample matrices. We will discuss them shortly. By the way, the correlation of fund A with fund B is the same as B with A. If N is the number of individual funds under consideration, the possible pairs of correlations is given by the expression $(N \times (N-1))/2$. A given fund always has a correlation of 1 with itself.

Our Investigation wants to examine the historical correlations of the individual funds we have chosen in step one so that we can be assured, when we get to the portfolio construction stage in step three, that we can assemble portfolios that are potentially diversified. If the constituent funds in a given portfolio are all highly and positively correlated, that is, tend to move together in the same direction, then we have not achieved the diversification we may have desired. A major source of Risk reduction has been compromised. If the funds we have assembled in step one are too highly correlated, we may want to revisit it to select alternative funds that enable us to achieve more diversification in the portfolios we'll construct in step three. Now, let's take a look at our two correlation matrices.

In Figure 1, we show the correlations between 6 mutual funds for one year, from 9.30.2009 to 9.30.2010. These examples represent 6 popular funds from a major fund family. There is no formal minimum agreed-upon level, that I am aware of, that indicates a serious threat to diversification. For me, .90 and above catches my attention, and .95 and above suggests that we may indeed have two funds that, at least for the time period in question, have tracked each other so closely that we may find a degree of diversification has been jeopardized. Notice that the lowest r between any 2 funds is .93. Notice that the highest r is actually 1.00, between funds 5 and 6! This is highly unusual, to say the least (I would guess it's due to rounding up). I also count 6 instances of r's of .99 or 1! Of the 15 possible pairs of correlations, fully 13 are at .95 or higher! It should be noted that these 6 funds are classified growth, growth and income, or equity income. There are no bond funds in this sample. Including such funds would certainly reveal some new, lower correlations, and possibly some negative ones. Nevertheless, if your portfolio consisted entirely of these 6 funds, it would be most difficult to claim it was diversified, at least for the one year in question.

Figure 1:   Major Fund Family One-Year Correlations
9.30.2009 through 9.30.2010

	Fund 1	Fund 2	Fund 3	Fund 4	Fund 5	Fund 6
Fund 1	1.00	0.99	0.97	0.93	0.93	0.95
Fund 2	0.99	1.00	0.98	0.95	0.95	0.96
Fund 3	0.97	0.98	1.00	0.97	0.99	0.99
Fund 4	0.93	0.95	0.97	1.00	0.99	0.99
Fund 5	0.93	0.95	0.99	0.99	1.00	1.00
Fund 6	0.95	0.96	0.99	0.99	1.00	1.00

Figure 2 consists of the same funds, but with a time period of 3 years. Fully 13 of the 15 possible correlations are .95 or higher! During the bear market of 2008, when the S&P 500 was down 37%, correlations of various investment categories increased and this fact may account to some extent for the elevated r's we see for this 3 year period. I included the 1 year data for comparison. This fund family may not necessarily represent an exception in terms of elevated correlations. I chose it to illustrate the importance of quantifying the degree of diversification an investor has assumed he or she has achieved in a given portfolio. You may be in for a surprise. Raise your hand if you like surprises.

Figure 2:   Major Fund Family Three-Year Correlations
9.30.2007 through 9.30.2010

	Fund 1	Fund 2	Fund 3	Fund 4	Fund 5	Fund 6
Fund 1	1.00	0.98	0.96	0.94	0.95	0.96
Fund 2	0.98	1.00	0.98	0.93	0.95	0.96
Fund 3	0.96	0.98	1.00	0.95	0.98	0.97
Fund 4	0.94	0.93	0.95	1.00	0.98	0.99
Fund 5	0.95	0.95	0.98	0.98	1.00	0.99
Fund 6	0.96	0.96	0.97	0.99	0.99	1.00

In the next chapter, we discuss the final step in the F.S.I. process, in which we assemble specific portfolios. That's what it's all about.

Chapter 5
F.S.I.: Portfolio Construction

In step three, we put it all together by creating portfolios comprised of the funds we selected in step one and further examined in step two to determine the extent of historical correlation between and among them. The portfolio becomes the basic unit of analysis.

Our initial selection of investment categories in step one obviously influences the individual funds we select and ultimately the composition of our portfolios. I emphasized the predilection of F.S.I. for funds with broader mandates, generally speaking. But when various categories focus on the same broad asset class, such as stocks, for example, we can expect some correlations between the funds ultimately selected to be relatively elevated. One of the most important considerations in the final portfolio construction process is to make sure, at least based on historical data, that this higher level of correlation is not pervasive throughout the final portfolio, if indeed you want to modulate Risk. By the way, you'll remember that in chapter 3, in which we discussed the screening process, we used a stock category as our example. DO NOT FORGET to add some bond funds to your mix of individual funds. The specific categories you choose are up to you and/or an experienced financial advisor. The categories I would strongly suggest you consider include, but needn't be limited to: multi-sector bond funds, global bond funds, short-term bond funds, intermediate-term bond funds, and adjustable-rate bond funds.

Step three requires specialized software that provides for each portfolio the statistics we relied upon in choosing the individual fund components. In other words, we will need to determine return and standard deviation (SD) for the portfolio as a whole. The software I use for the F.S.I. process backtests each portfolio for 1, 3, 5, and 10 year periods. It provides SD for all periods except 1 year. It also provides some additional MPT statistics: Sharpe Ratio, Alpha, Beta, and R-squared. Of these additional stats, only R-squared concerns us here. It also allows for the use of a benchmark index that enables us to compare the above statistics generated by our portfolio with the respective values generated by the index. I use the S&P 500 as the benchmark for my growth portfolios and the Barclays Capital US Aggregate Bond Index for my income portfolios. We will discuss indexes more fully in Chapter 9, but at this point it would be helpful to explain their function in step three of my F.S.I. process.

Beating or tracking an index is definitely not a goal of F.S.I. The inclusion of the two indexes referred to above serves several purposes. I want to know how our portfolios compare with these benchmarks primarily in terms of return and SD (Risk, remember!). Not just for the typical 3, 5, and 10 year spans, as constituted at any given time, but how these comparisons play out over succeeding months, since I like to update these portfolios monthly. In a way, it is reminiscent of the ancient mariners' use of the North Star to keep their ships on course: are our portfolios straying off course with respect to the return and Risk numbers of our chosen benchmark indexes? Do our portfolios increasingly lag their respective benchmarks in terms of return, and are they approaching or even surpassing their respective benchmarks in terms of Risk? I'd like to know. We'll refer to this topic later. And, by the way, because many investors have some general sense of the Risk associated with the stock market simply through witnessing its ongoing gyrations, comparing the SD of our growth portfolios with the SD of our stock market proxy, the S&P 500, serves to differentiate them in more concrete, comprehensible terms.

***

In a sense, the actual construction process involves some degree of trial and error. And judgment. There are no right or wrong or "perfect" portfolios. Begin with a general characterization of objective: conservative growth, moderate growth, moderate-aggressive growth, aggressive growth, conservative income, moderate income, aggressive income, and so on. While you may characterize these portfolios with the adjectives "conservative," "moderate," "aggressive," and so on, the SD's associated with each portfolio will be the final determinant of Risk level. The goal: Construct portfolios that vary by historical level of Risk and return. How they compare with the benchmarks you have chosen (they are not required to be the same as mine!) will be revealed each time you run the software. Do you want to beat the 500 for 1, 3, 5, and 10 years in terms of return? How much Risk will you accept in so doing? Is it necessary for your portfolios to register lower historical levels of Risk than your chosen benchmarks? The answers to these questions derive from your own personal objectives, Risk tolerances, and, ultimately, time horizons. Discussing these questions and considerations with an experienced financial advisor may well be indicated. In any case, a certain amount of judgment must necessarily enter into these deliberations. The numbers alone will not suffice. This is not necessarily a bad thing.

Begin with the collection of funds assembled in step one. In step two, you'll remember, we tested for the degree of diversification offered by this collection. We suggested that if the correlation matrix of these funds revealed a very high degree of correlation, you should consider substituting some of the funds with new selections to enable our ultimate portfolios to be more diversified. Of course, to some extent, the degree of diversification in our final portfolios will be reflected in the SD's associated with them. We have essentially three decisions to make as we assemble potential portfolios: (1) How many funds do we include in a given portfolio? (2) Which funds do we use? and (3) How do we weight them?

A revolutionary process known as trial and error works wonders in this context. However, what we are actually employing is F.S.I.-enhanced trial and error (FSI-ET&E). After all, we know the historical returns, SD's and correlations of our individual funds, and, to some extent, can modify the return and Risk characteristics of the portfolios we are constructing. Yet we can only guess at these characteristics, because we don't know how the constituent funds we have chosen for any given trial will interact with each other to determine the portfolio's final numbers, until we have actually run them through our software. Also, as previously mentioned, the desirability of the final numbers generated by each iteration of fund combinations is highly dependent on our ultimate goals for each portfolio.

A few words about choosing the final number of funds in each portfolio and how they are weighted. Using the aforementioned FSI-ET&E, you can see for yourself how the numbers change as funds are added and their weightings changed. On principle, in any case, I would use no more funds per portfolio than needed to meet your objectives. Concentrate on the 3 year numbers, but do pay attention to the 5 and 10 year stats. Take a look, as well, at the 1 year numbers to get a feel for how the portfolio has reacted to a more recent set of circumstances. Keep in mind, too, that screening for a manager tenure of three or more years does not in itself guarantee that he/she will have been at the helm for the longer time periods, though some additional research can confirm that rather easily. Also, it is conceivable that the current manager may have been involved with the fund previously in another capacity, suggesting, but not guaranteeing, some continuity of style from previous periods. In any case, a pattern of lower SD's than the benchmark you use may indicate some continuity of management style, but again, not guarantee it. I weight funds in multiples of 5%, just to keep things simpler. I'm not sure any finer differentiations are worth the effort in terms of improved effectiveness. You may have to enter your weightings in dollar terms, in which case I suggest simply assuming a total of $100 per portfolio, and assigning weights accordingly.

DO NOT HESITATE TO USE THE SAME FUNDS IN MULTIPLE PORTFOLIOS. After all, if you've found an attractive fund/capable manager, why not take advantage of the fact and use it/he/she multiple times? Simply weight the fund in accordance with the objective of each portfolio. And don't be afraid to add a bond fund(s) to a growth portfolio. At the time of this writing, my three growth portfolios and two income portfolios are comprised of a total of only 16 different funds. Some are indeed used only once, most multiple times. This is not to say that in the future I will not add funds to bring the total above 16, or remove a fund or funds because I can replace them with a more attractive fund in a given category. In any case, fewer constituent funds means fewer funds to keep tabs on. Currently, my three growth portfolios contain 8 funds each. My conservative income portfolio contains 6 funds and my moderate income portfolio contains 5.

Don't forget to keep an eye on the managers of your chosen funds. A departure may be quite significant for the fate of the fund. In some cases, you may find that an assistant manager or managers have remained, and continue to run the fund similarly to the lead manager who has left. You may find it useful to discuss the matter with the fund family sponsoring the fund. In any case, keep your eyes open. In fact, you need to follow all the funds you have originally selected, not only for manager change, but simply a change of approach or any other factor that may cause future numbers to deviate from the pattern you have detected in your historical analysis.

Don't forget to keep track of the correlation matrix of the funds in each of your final portfolios. This obviously doesn't need to be done daily. Increasing correlations mean decreasing diversification. Certainly, if the correlations among several funds increase significantly, and one of the funds happens to perform particularly well, then we would expect the others to follow to some degree. This is good. However, if you could reliably predict when to have a less diversified portfolio by concentrating in certain more highly correlated funds, you wouldn't need this book. The more the number of investors who could accomplish this feat, the less demand there would be for my book. That's called an inverse, or negative, correlation.

Figure 3, which follows, consists of the summary data associated with my five model portfolios. Data are as of 9.30.2010. The variable of manager tenure can be complex. As mentioned above, when a manager leaves a fund, it is possible that a co-manager or other colleague(s) can maintain continuity of style. I am aware of some cases among my funds in which a manager has left direct management of the fund. The exact circumstances vary, and we need not concern ourselves with the details. All funds remain, as of the time of this writing, in their respective portfolios. Let's assume, for the purpose of analyzing the following statistics, that consistency of management style across the constituent funds cannot be guaranteed for the time periods shown. Nevertheless, I believe the data generally may well be significant, and that, in any case, Figure 3 may serve as a template for you when you construct your own portfolios based on my F.S.I. process. Remember too, that past statistics are no guarantee of future statistics, for these, or any, portfolios, and that these numbers represent the results from backtesting hypothetical portfolios that have not actually existed for the time periods shown.

On to chapter 6, and more about the good things that numbers can offer you.

Figure 3: F.S.I. Model Portfolios Data

	3 years		5 years		10 years	
	P	B	P	B	P	B
Conservative Income						
Return (%)	8.29	7.41	7.58	6.20	7.29	6.41
Std Dev (%)	3.17	4.14	2.70	3.60	2.66	3.80
R-Squared	0.31		0.36		0.47	
Moderate Income						
Return (%)	10.13	7.41	8.85	6.20	8.46	6.41
Std Dev (%)	4.31	4.14	3.69	3.60	3.71	3.80
R-Squared	0.38		0.43		0.56	
Conservative Growth						
Return (%)	3.84	-7.16	7.00	0.64	8.40	-0.43
Std Dev (%)	9.65	21.81	7.98	17.61	6.79	16.41
R-Squared	0.79		0.75		0.64	
Moderate Growth						
Return (%)	2.14	-7.16	7.40	0.64	8.95	-0.43
Std Dev (%)	12.14	21.81	10.16	17.61	8.73	16.41
R-Squared	0.81		0.77		0.68	
Moderate Aggressive Growth						
Return (%)	1.23	-7.16	7.73	0.64	9.54	-0.43
Std Dev (%)	16.63	21.81	13.99	17.61	11.90	16.41
R-Squared	0.77		0.72		0.66	

NOTES: The "P" and "B" columns provide values for the specified portfolios and their benchmarks, respectively. The benchmark for the Income portfolios is the Barclays Capital US Aggregate Bond Index. For the Growth portfolios, the benchmark is the S&P 500. All data are as of 9.30.2010.

Chapter 6
"Show Me the Numbers"

The theme that things are not always as they appear in the world of investments was first presented in the Introduction to this book. And we revisit it now. It is a recurrent theme in the philosophical/theoretical foundation of F.S.I. This chapter suggests techniques for comparing appearance and reality, as our Investigation continues.

You explained to your financial advisor/planner that you wanted him/her to construct a growth portfolio with moderate Risk and a conservative income portfolio. You have been reading about bonds and bond funds and discovered that rising interest rates normally depress bond prices. So you further instructed him/her to take this fact into account. He calls and tells you he's all set, and you schedule an appointment to meet.

He assures you the growth portfolio is moderate in terms of Risk (though neither of you really spelled out what this meant). He assures you the portfolio is nicely diversified to modulate Risk. Likewise, your income portfolio is duly conservative (though neither of you really spelled out what this meant). He also assures you that he has taken your concern about rising interest rates into account. Needless to say, this portfolio is nicely diversified as well.

He shows you the constituent funds of each portfolio. And indeed, it looks as if the growth portfolio is effectively diversified. Not only are the funds targeting very different investment categories, they are sponsored by completely different fund families. The same applies to your income portfolio. Everything looks in order, and you thank him for his diligence. Things in the world of investments very often look in order. But very often it's wise to take a closer look, perhaps from a different angle or perspective. So before you leave, I'd like to suggest four words to communicate to your advisor: "SHOW ME THE NUMBERS!" (Actually, you don't have to shout).

Take a look at the standard deviations of the growth portfolio over various time intervals. How do they compare to the S&P 500's SD's over those same periods? If the Risk is approximately the same, is this what you meant by moderate? Was the Risk higher in your portfolio? If so, were the returns commensurate with this elevated Risk? The portfolio seems to be diversified, but why not see if your advisor can show you a correlation matrix of these funds, so you can actually view the numbers? By the way, it might be interesting to see how closely the portfolio as a whole tracks the 500. Remember R-squared?

Let's turn to your income portfolio. Remember, bond funds are not riskless. Take a look at the SD's of your income portfolio over various periods. You might want to compare it to the Barclay's Aggregate referred to earlier. This index consists of various kinds of US dollar investment grade bonds, that are fixed rate, non-convertible, with at least one year to maturity. Has your portfolio experienced more Risk? How about the returns? Also, you may want to compare the numbers with the S&P 500, to get some idea of the relative historical Risk. Remember, one advantage of using SD is that you can compare historical Risk levels of completely different portfolios. Don't forget to ask your advisor what the current distribution rate looks like for your income portfolio. After all, you're buying this portfolio for the income.

Don't forget your concern about the exposure of your income portfolio to rising interest rates. There is a statistic known as duration which measures the sensitivity of a bond or bond mutual fund or portfolio to movements of interest rates. The higher the number the more sensitive the portfolio is to rate moves, both up and down. A portfolio with a duration of 8 (years) is considered to lose approximately 8% in value for every 1 percentage point increase in rates, and to gain approximately 8% for every 1 percentage point decline in rates. Ask your advisor for the duration of your income portfolio.

The numbers are available, so you may as well get them. After all, sometimes portfolios are full of surprises. You may have to schedule another meeting. Sorry.

Our Investigation proceeds to chapter 7, in which we show you more numbers. And share with you a basic principle relating to investing on planet Earth. Seriously.

Chapter 7
Risk Matters

WARNING! In this chapter we confront RISK head-on. It won't be pretty. But neither is the alternative: You can run, but you can't hide. As promised, there're more numbers, as we take a look at an actual fund, its returns, and its Risk.

The fund is the Legg Mason CM Value Trust. We will be looking at the most popular share class, based on assets: the C shares, ticker LMVTX. The fund has been managed since its inception by Bill Miller, who guided it to a record 15 consecutive years of beating the S&P 500, an amazing feat. The string came to an end in 2006. You can understand, however, that this remarkable accomplishment could well have made for a convincing buy recommendation.

In calendar year 2008, LMVTX lost just over 55%. To get back to what industry insiders call even, you must follow such a loss with a subsequent gain of approximately 122%. In that same year, the S&P 500 lost 37%. In absolute terms, LMVTX trailed the 500 by approximately 18%. In relative terms, by approximately 50%! As of 9.30.2010, LMVTX had sustained a 3-yr annualized loss of 17.20%, a 5-yr annualized loss of 8.09% and a 10-yr annualized loss of 3.14%. The respective numbers for the S&P 500 were minus 7.16%, plus 0.64%, and minus 0.43%. Those numbers, of course, include calendar year 2009, when LMVTX returned +40.64% vs. the 500's +26.46%! One year back from 9.30.2010: LMVTX gained 2.15% and the 500 gained 10.17%. Is there a point here? What do you think?

Was there any sort of warning that this fund could reverse course so markedly? Our Investigation may have just stumbled upon a clue. Let's check it out: Namely, what do the historical levels of Risk look like for this fund? Here are the 1, 3, 5, and 10yr annualized standard deviations for LMVTX: 21.20%, 31.16%, 25.38%, and 23.03%. These numbers, again, are back from 9.30.2010. Corresponding numbers for the 500: 18.69%, 22.69%, 18.32%, and 17.02%. Respectively, LMVTX was approximately 13%, 37%, 39%, and 35% riskier than the S&P 500.

LMVTX vs. S&P 500

	1 yr	3 yr	5 yr	10 yr
Return LMVTX (%)	2.15	-17.20	-8.09	-3.14
Return S&P 500 (%)	10.17	-7.16	0.64	-0.43
SD LMVTX (%)	21.20	31.16	25.38	23.03
SD S&P 500 (%)	18.69	22.69	18.32	17.02

The point is that by examining historical Risk metrics, particularly over various time intervals, we may be able to detect a pattern. You'll remember that standard deviation is an absolute measure of Risk, but that doesn't mean we can't compare it to an index with which we have some familiarity. For most investors this would be the Dow 30 or the S&P 500. It is helpful to know if a fund we are considering buying has been riskier than a broad market index like the 500. Obviously any pattern that emerges may not necessarily repeat itself in future years, any more than past performance is a guarantee of future returns. But patterns are often a good place to start. Can we find a clue or clues explaining the relatively elevated Risk of the Value Trust? Let's proceed to the Legg Mason web site.

As of 9.30.2010, the financial sector comprised 25.10% of the fund and the information technology sector, 23.30%. These two sectors comprised almost 50% of the fund. If these sectors performed well from this point, the fund could have the wind at its back, so to speak. However, difficulties in these sectors could generate a difficult headwind. As of 4.30.2010, the above sectors comprised 28.1% and 27.3% respectively. As of 10.31.2009, these sectors comprised 26.6% and 28.6% respectively. It is possible that the concentration in just two sectors could account for much of the heightened Risk. In any case, the SD's speak for themselves.

Get in the habit of checking out past Risk levels of funds you are considering. If the levels seem particularly elevated, try to determine why. Higher levels of Risk do not necessarily mean you should avoid the fund entirely, if the returns have at times been attractive. Also, the fund might provide a degree of diversification through its potentially lower correlation with some of your existing positions. You might decide to invest 5% of available assets therein, instead of the 10% you were considering. And while you're at it, you may as well check out R-squared's, manager tenures, etc., as described in Chapter 3. Just keep your eyes open! By the way, since inception in 1982, the LM Value Trust has a positive annualized return of 11.65%, as of 9.30.2010.

Now for that basic principle I promised you. It's about how Risk works on planet Earth. It is as follows: If you prosper by taking a lot of Risk, sooner or later you will likely deprosper. The Legg Mason Value Trust deprospered in 2008 by over 55%. I have no idea how Risk works on Jupiter, Mars, or Venus. Maybe one day we'll find out.

Before we board our starship, let's discuss allocation, in chapter 8.

Chapter 8
Allocation, Allocation, Allocation: Allocation by Objective

As location is a basic factor in the world of retail, so is allocation in the world of investing. We have not allocated a great deal of space to the concept *per se,* though we have discussed the existence of various investment categories, which comprise the building blocks, if you will, of the allocation process. This process typically constructs portfolios by including a set of investment categories, which may vary from investor to investor, weighted according to certain assumptions, the weights, once again, varying from investor to investor. If the portfolio builder, be it a wirehouse, a financial advisor, or an individual investor, believes that the world economy will surge soon, a higher weighting may be given to energy and materials sectors, as well as industrial sectors, and a lower weighting to more defensive sectors like healthcare and consumer products. And don't forget categories such as large-cap value, mid-cap growth, small-cap value, international equity, long-term investment grade corporates, emerging market bonds, etc., as additional building blocks. You can see how the process can become quite complex, quite rapidly.

But there are other criteria on which to base the allocation process. Risk is certainly one of them, and indeed is intrinsically built into the category selection and weighting process (either intentionally or accidentally). But a more inclusive and perhaps more useful criterion is objective. In other words, you allocate your investment dollars based upon what you want to achieve with them. And each objective is represented by a discrete portfolio. I see, simply, two primary objectives: Growth and Income. These objectives may be divided into secondary ones based on level of Risk. Thus we may have a conservative growth objective, a moderate-Risk growth objective, and an aggressive growth objective, as well as a conservative income objective, a moderate-Risk income objective, and conceivably, an aggressive income objective. Other objectives that you can think of, such as college funding and retirement, can generally be subsumed under one or a combination of the above secondary objectives. Keep in mind, too, that while we may use the descriptors conservative, moderate, aggressive, and even moderate-aggressive, we are really referring to ranges of historical SD's. Your conservative may be my moderate, and her aggressive may be his moderate, but with standard deviation we are all on the same page. When you are investing your own dollars with your financial advisor, it is so much better to be on the same page (you have probably already reached the conclusion that the same page doesn't get the credit or recognition it deserves)!

By discrete portfolios, ultimately I am referring to separate brokerage accounts. This enables each portfolio to be managed and evaluated separately, which makes both processes much more efficient and less confusing. With objectives more clearly defined, managing each portfolio is much simpler. If your objectives change, the weighting of the respective portfolio can be adjusted, or the portfolio can even be liquidated and the proceeds distributed among the remaining objectives. This approach is at the heart of the F.S.I. process. It also enables significant flexibility and encourages a clearer understanding of what you are trying to accomplish with your investment dollars. Let's take a look at a specific example related to retirement planning.

You and your financial advisor have determined that for the first year of retirement you and your spouse will need approximately $5000 per month to meet your expenses. This figure was derived from adding up all your non-discretionary expenses, such as mortgage payments, auto insurance, health insurance, utilities, food, etc., plus some additional provision for some basic discretionary expenses, such as dining out, an occasional vacation, etc. For future years, consider an adjustment for inflation. Then, revenues such as social security payments, pension payments, current investment income, etc., were subtracted. The remainder was adjusted for taxes, leaving a figure of $2500. Producing this amount on a monthly basis would seem to be a worthy objective. So consider creating an income portfolio dedicated to producing the desired amount. Or maybe even two income portfolios, one somewhat riskier with a higher duration, to produce additional income if the desired amount cannot be achieved with the first, more conservative portfolio. And remember to ask your advisor to show you the numbers. And don't forget to factor in, at some point, IRA or other retirement plan distributions, whether you wait until they are required or begin them sooner.

This approach, building a portfolio or portfolios dedicated to producing income to satisfy ongoing expenses, is entirely consonant with the F.S.I. process, but derives from a concept known as Liability-Driven Investing, practiced for some years now by pension plans. It certainly makes sense at the individual investor level. Obviously, sufficient investment dollars may not exist to produce the desired amount of revenue from the fixed income side only. This means that additional Risk may have to be assumed via a portfolio or portfolios with a growth objective. But to the extent that fixed income funding exists, reliance on riskier growth portfolios is reduced. If sufficient funding exists to derive the required level of revenue from a fixed income portfolio(s), and there are funds remaining, then said funds can be directed toward growth objectives, with the knowledge that, if so desired, additional levels of Risk than would otherwise be comfortable could be assumed, because basic recurring liabilities are covered. This is in some respects a simple concept, yet also a very powerful one. Don't forget, in this context, when you see the word "portfolio," think "account."

Allocation by objective is a simple concept. It is also a powerful one.

And one more point about managing portfolios separately. It facilitates rebalancing, a process by which your original fund weightings are restored after a period of time. Obviously fund weightings will vary as market conditions vary. You may consider rebalancing when these deviations reach a prescribed percentage, or on a predetermined schedule: every six months or one year, for example. By returning your constituent funds to their original proportions, within portfolios, you are replicating the weightings which you used to generate the portfolio originally. Keep in mind that the underlying metrics of your funds and portfolios are continually changing, which is why I recommend periodically updating each portfolio. Also, don't forget, if your objectives change, rebalancing can occur between and among portfolios! This allocation approach yields significant flexibility. You should discuss rebalancing with your financial advisor.

Our Investigation continues with a discussion of index investing, an extremely popular topic in the financial press.

Chapter 9
The Only Index That Matters

I have referred to market indexes quite often in preceding chapters. By comparing the SD's of the various portfolios you may create with the SD of a relevant index with which you have some familiarity, the extent of the portfolio's historical Risk becomes more meaningful. For instance, if you are uncomfortable with the Risk associated with the market as measured by the S&P 500, you would want to weight a given portfolio more heavily if its Risk was less than the 500's. That does not preclude some weighting in a portfolio that has approximated the 500's, or even exceeded it, over various historical timeframes. The point is, by comparing the historical Risk of the portfolios you and/or your advisor construct with a meaningfully relevant index, you can assemble an overall investment strategy that, at least based on historical data, is more consonant with your personal Risk tolerance. Quantifying Risk makes it more meaningful and comprehensible. Comparing the Risk that you are contemplating, or are willing to assume, with that of a relevant, broad market index, enhances your understanding and appreciation of it. We have also mentioned returns of portfolios in relation to relevant indexes. This, once again, serves to anchor your expectations in regard to return potential. And, as mentioned, I use indexes as fixed reference points in evaluating my portfolios as I update their metrics periodically.

There has been a great deal of discussion in the financial press about the relative merits of active management vs.

passive (index) investing. This discussion and the research upon which it is based, can get rather complex. In any case, it need not concern us here, the reason for which I shall disclose shortly. Suffice it to say, that there are numerous examples of actively managed funds trailing their respective indexes, but also examples of the opposite can readily be found. While this issue is not relevant to our Investigation, certainly it has academic merit, and is highly relevant in certain contexts.

If tracking an index with your investments is important to you, it's really quite difficult to mount an argument against buying an index fund or appropriate ETF. Based on the philosophy supporting the F.S.I. process, it's really quite difficult to understand why you would want to track an index. Think about the nature of an index, if you will. There is a certain arbitrariness to any investment index. Who's to say what the appropriate number of stocks (or bonds) is in any index? And how to weight the index components? To simplify matters, let's confine our attention to stock indexes. Many are cap-weighted, which means the constituent companies are weighted based on their capitalization (share price times number of shares outstanding). Why not weight the components equally? After deciding how many stocks in a given index, and how to weight them, how do we choose the stocks themselves? Obviously these questions have been answered many times over, based on the number of indexes in existence. In any case, the question bears repeating: why track an index no matter how it's constructed?

Investors tracking the 500 in 2008 were down about 37%. Returning to the *status quo ante* required an upward move of almost 59%. Remember, no matter how you define them, indexes are always fully invested. And if you're tracking them via an index fund, so are you. I would not expect to find many investors with all their dollars in one index fund, but even as you diversify among other indexes you are still held hostage to each, both in terms of Risk and return. And don't forget that the Russell 2000 Growth Index has no place to hide when things look unpleasant for its small cap companies and the MSCI Emerging Markets Index must remain fully exposed to emerging market stocks even if their developed market trading partners experience plummeting demand for their exports. I'm not claiming that an actively managed fund can sidestep these unfortunate circumstances on a consistent basis, but having the flexibility to underweight certain sectors from time to time may be useful, from time to time. When you combine this discretionary ability on the part of a given fund manager with that of other managers in the same portfolio, you may very well facilitate the opportunity to reduce Risk, though I'm not certain this can be specifically proven. Remember, our initial screening process focuses on choosing managers who have demonstrated the ability to modulate Risk.

I'm not suggesting indexes are a threat to the investment world's ecosystem, or need to be outlawed. In fact, if indexes are transparently constructed and consistently maintained over time, they can be useful instruments to track sector and category returns, Risk, and correlations over time. Such data can be useful as indicators of change in the investment world's ecosystem, and perhaps, accordingly, reveal new and useful strategic insights. For example, if an analysis suggests an increasing correlation of an emerging market stock index with an index of US industrial stocks over time, a subsequent investigation may disclose a significant, new factor at work (or not), which could further provide useful information from an economic and/or business perspective. If we notice the standard deviation of an index tracking the US consumer discretionary sector increasing over a time period when many other US stock sector indexes are not behaving similarly, perhaps this fact may hold relevant implications for the retail sector (or not). The above argument however in no way suggests that there is anything to be gained from tracking an index or combination of indexes with your investment dollars. In fact, there may be much to lose.

Let me conclude by fulfilling the promise implied in the title of this chapter. There does indeed exist an index that you would indeed be advised to track, the more closely the better, the foregoing discussion notwithstanding. It is the MPGI. You will not find it listed or updated daily in the Wall Street Journal or any other financial publication, due to space constraints. MPGI stands for "My Personal Goals Index." Tracking this index is ultimately the only reason for you to invest and, trust me, it is the ONLY INDEX THAT MATTERS.

"Logic will get you from A to B. Imagination will take you everywhere."

Albert Einstein

At this point in time, I like to think the F.S.I. process consists of 3 parts logic to 1 part imagination. I intend to maintain that "allocation" for the foreseeable future.

"Those who cannot remember the past are condemned to repeat it."

George Santayana

Followers of F.S.I. should like nothing better than for the past to repeat itself: We've got a great many of the relevant numbers. Unfortunately the past, like the markets, cannot be relied upon in this way. So I suggest ongoing monitoring of your portfolios after the initial construction phase.

Chapter 10
Concluding Reflections

As our Investigation concludes, let's retrace some of our steps.

We began with an introduction to the F.S.I. ("Fund Screen Investigation") process and the investment philosophy from which it derives. The foundational assumption is that, as investors, the only thing we can control is our exposure to Risk. No one has been able to consistently outguess any market with respect to timing or sector allocation. Another theme that accompanied our Investigation was that things are not always as they appear in the world of investments. So keep your eyes open and focused on the numbers! Indeed, a major goal of F.S.I. is to provide you a new perspective to assist you in this mission. However, the ultimate goal of F.S.I. is to construct portfolios that vary by historical level of Risk and return. The process is highly structured, quantitative, and based, in part, on Modern Portfolio Theory statistics and concepts.

Our Investigation continued with a discussion of the nature of Risk as defined and measured by standard deviation. We then progressed to an examination of the three steps that comprise the F.S.I. process: initial screening to select the individual component funds, correlating these funds to ensure that a sufficient degree of diversification can be achieved when they are combined into portfolios, and actually constructing these portfolios by back-testing successive iterations of various combinations and weightings of the individual funds to create structured portfolios differentiated by historical Risk and return. We noted, however, that because the essence of Risk lies in its futurity, F.S.I. strongly suggests that these portfolios be evaluated on an ongoing basis.

We then discussed a hypothetical scenario that illustrated the rationale behind the "Show Me the Numbers" mandate, basic to the F.S.I. process. Our Investigation then uncovered a real-life example of what can befall an investor who ignores one of those numbers in particular: Standard Deviation.

We next suggested that allocating your investment dollars by objective, in separate portfolios, makes good sense. Portfolios that have precisely defined objectives can be more efficiently managed and evaluated than portfolios in which many objectives are commingled. Separate portfolios also facilitate periodic rebalancing.

The final stage of our Investigation argued against investing to track any given index, with the sole exception being the MPGI.

Though our Investigation is concluding, never forget that when you invest, your Investigation must remain ongoing.

And one last thing. If you truly believe, deep in your heart, that Risk matters, please raise your hand!

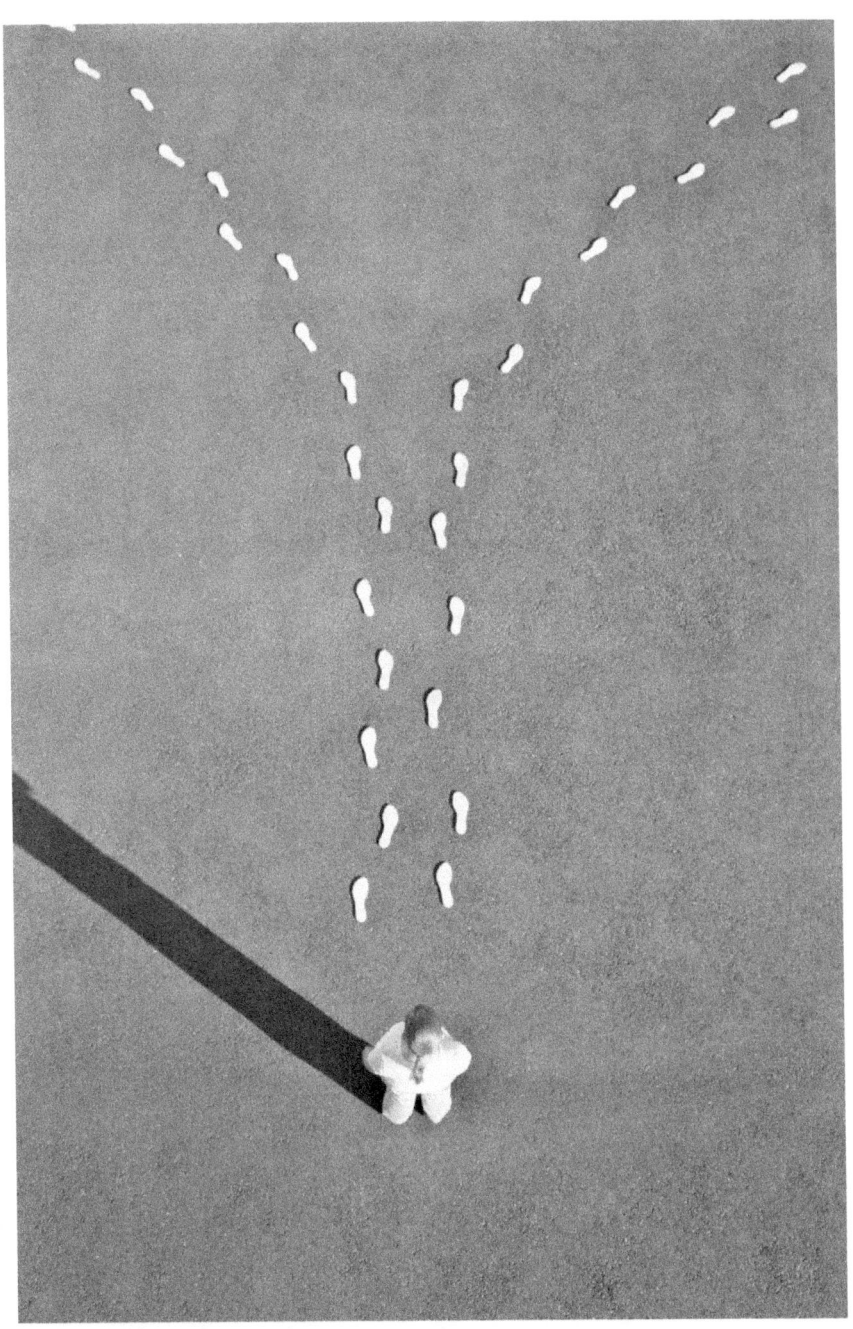

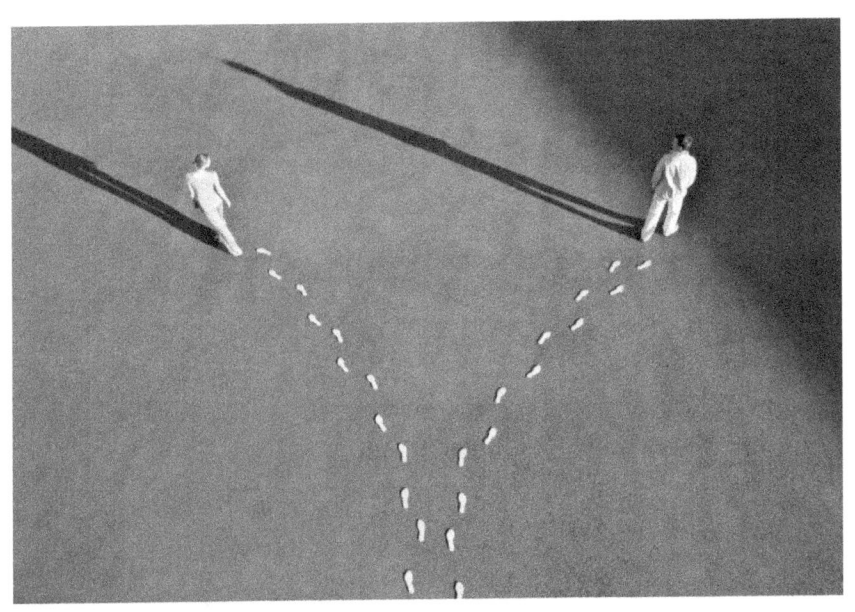

www.ingramcontent.com/pod-product-compliance
Lightning Source LLC
Chambersburg PA
CBHW051236170526
45165CB00004B/1456